COUNTRIES OF THE WORLD

Nepal

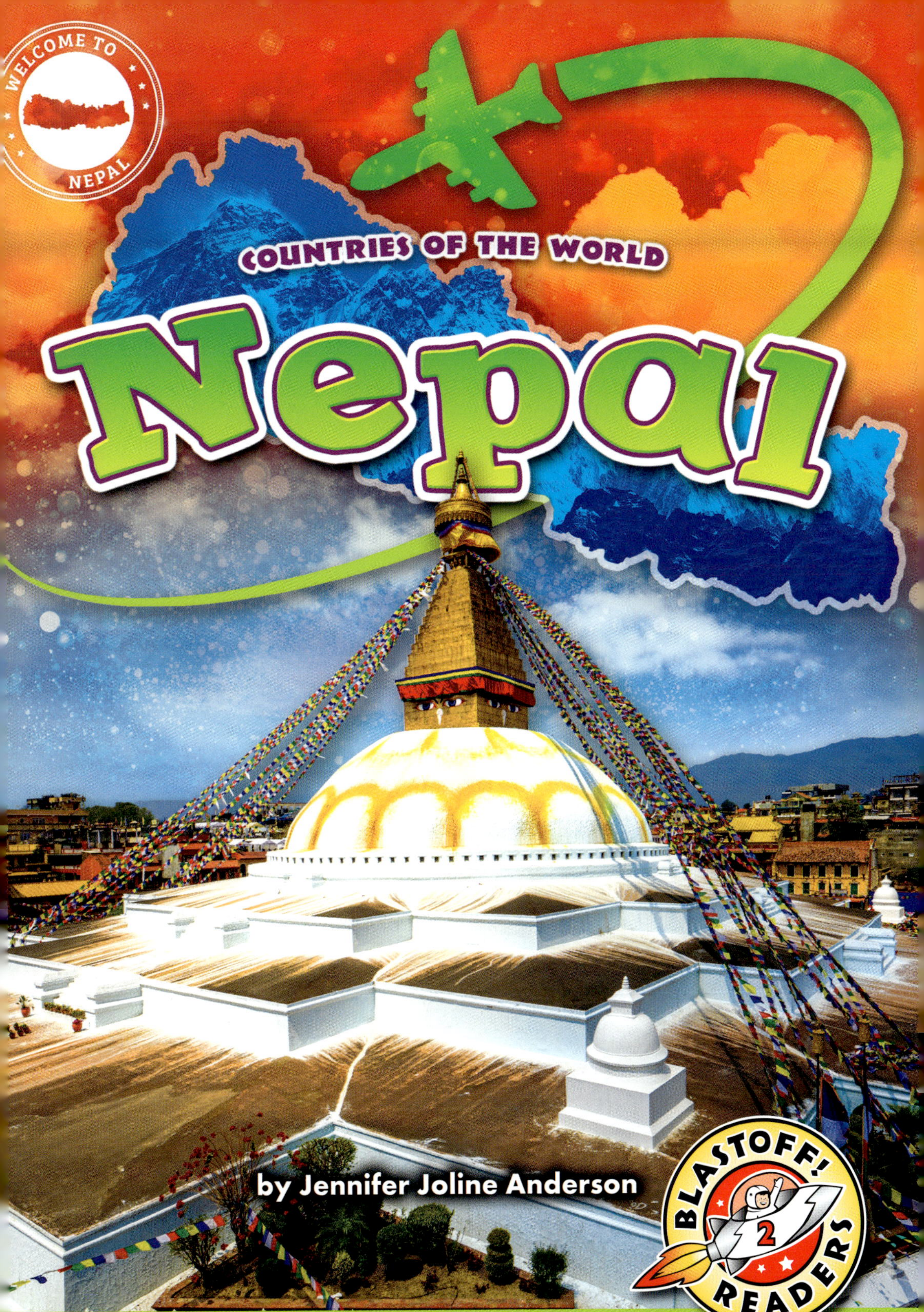

by Jennifer Joline Anderson

BLASTOFF! READERS, AN IMPRINT OF BELLWETHER MEDIA BY FLUTTERBEE

Blastoff! Readers are carefully developed by literacy experts to build reading stamina and move students toward fluency by combining standards-based content with developmentally appropriate text.

LEVELS

Level 1 provides the most support through repetition of high-frequency words, light text, predictable sentence patterns, and strong visual support.

Level 2 offers early readers a bit more challenge through varied sentences, increased text load, and text-supportive special features.

Level 3 advances early-fluent readers toward fluency through increased text load, less reliance on photos, advancing concepts, longer sentences, and more complex special features.

★ **Blastoff! Universe**

Reading Level

Blastoff! Beginners — Grade K

Blastoff! Readers — Grades 1–3

Blastoff! Discovery — Grade 4

This edition first published in 2027 by Bellwether Media, Inc.

For information regarding permission, write to Bellwether Media, Inc., Attention: Permissions Department, 3500 American Blvd W, Suite 150, Bloomington, MN 55431.

Library of Congress Cataloging-in-Publication Data is available at www.loc.gov or upon request from the publisher.

ISBN: 9798898800475 (hardcover)
ISBN: 9798898801717 (ebook)

Editor: Betsy Rathburn Designer: Laura Sowers

Printed in the United States of America, North Mankato, MN.

Table of Contents

All About Nepal

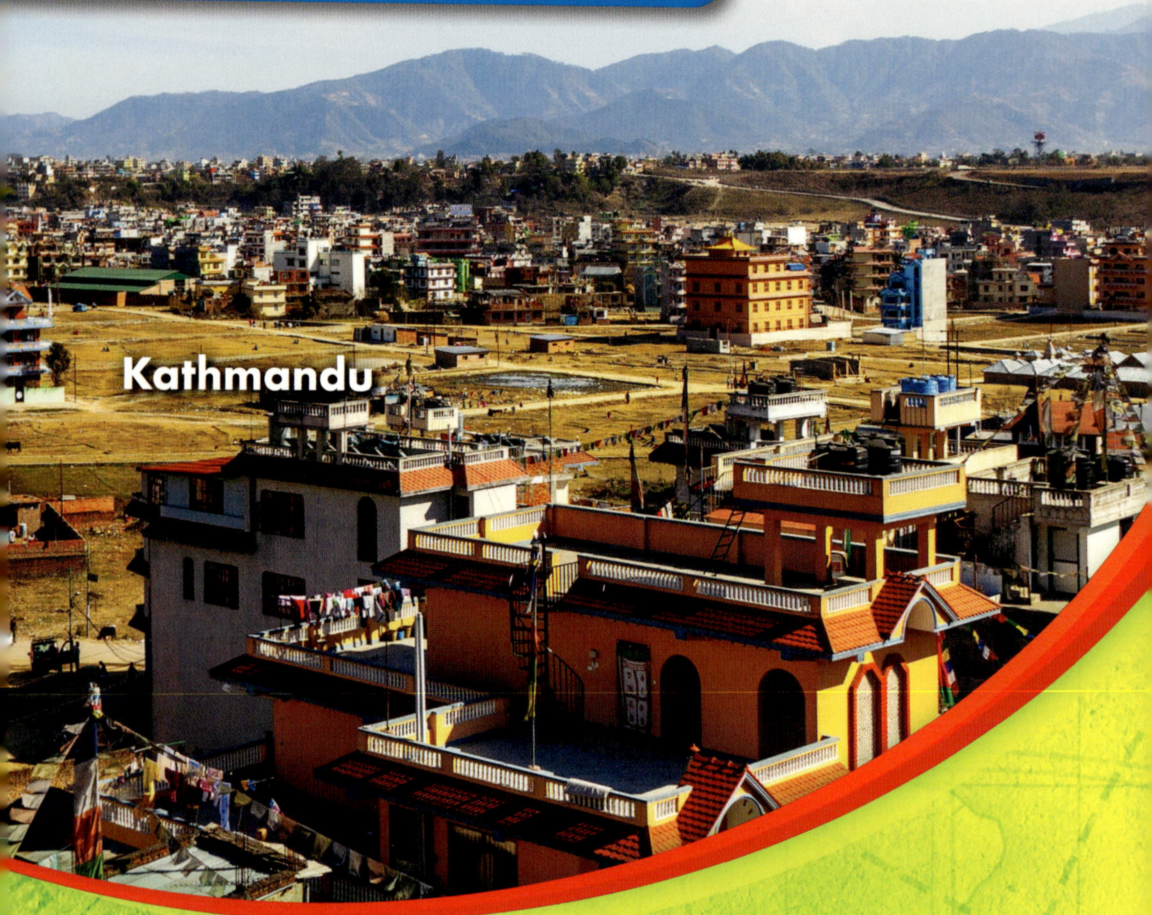

Nepal is a country in South Asia. Kathmandu is its capital.

The Himalayas run through Nepal. This mountain **range** has many peaks!

Land and Animals

In the north, snow and **glaciers** cover mountain peaks. Forests grow in hills and valleys.

Flat **plains** lie in the south. Rivers flow into lakes.

plains

Mount Everest

Size: 29,032 feet (8,849 meters) tall

Famous For: the tallest mountain on Earth's surface

Mountain weather is freezing.
In the lowlands, the weather is hot.

The **monsoon** season is from June through September. Heavy rains fall.

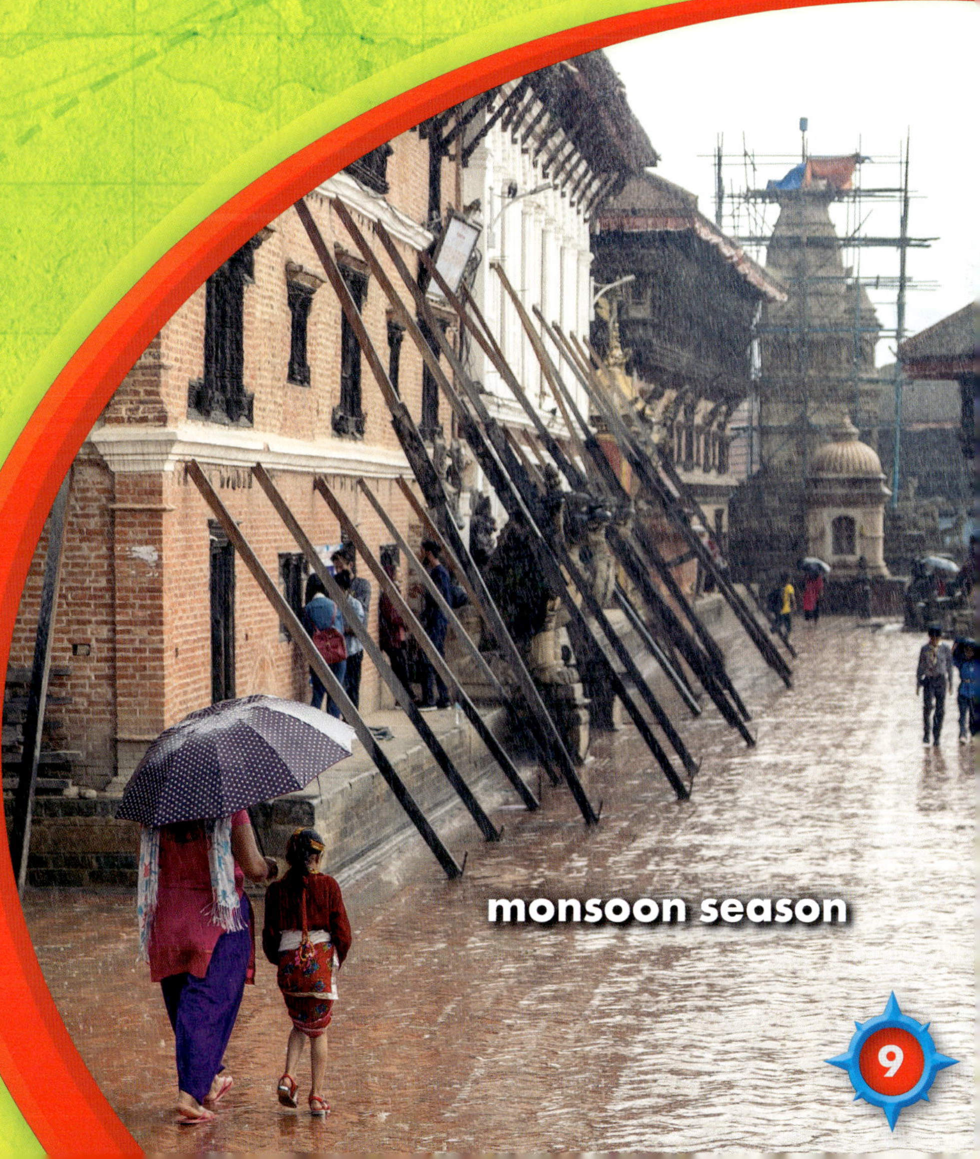

monsoon season

Snow leopards hunt for blue sheep in the mountains. Gharials eat fish in rivers.

Himalayan monal

Animals of Nepal

snow leopard

gharial

red panda

Indian pangolin

Red pandas and pangolins hide in forests. The Himalayan monal is the national bird.

Life in Nepal

Most people live in villages. Kathmandu is the biggest city.

More than 120 languages are spoken in Nepal. Nepali is the main language.

English: Hello
Nepali: Namaste
(nah-mah-STAY)

Folk music and dancing are valued **traditions**. Wood carving is a popular hobby. Soccer is the most popular sport.

Many people visit **temples**. Some people **trek** in the mountains.

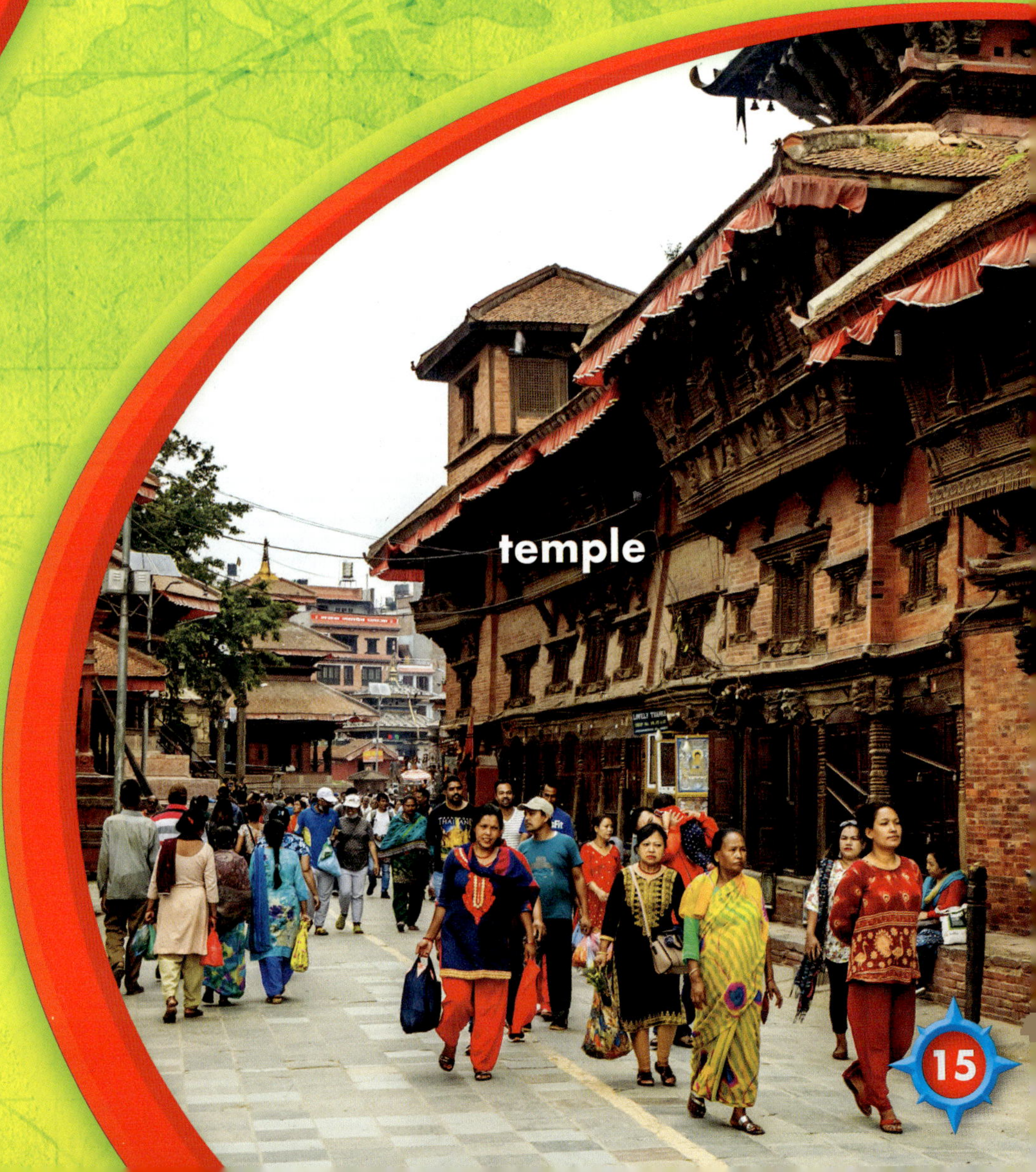

Dal bhat has rice, lentils, and vegetables. *Momos* are meat dumplings.

Nepali Foods

dal bhat

momos

thukpa

sel roti

Thukpa is a noodle soup.
Sel roti are sweet rice doughnuts.

Dashain is a **Hindu** holiday. Families fly kites. They swing on tall swings.

Tihar is the **festival** of lights. People light candles and lamps. Nepali people love to **celebrate** their **culture**!

Tihar

Dashain

Nepal Facts

Size:
56,827 square miles
(147,181 square kilometers)

Population:
31,122,387 (2024)

National Holiday:
Constitution Day (September 19)

Main Language:
Nepali

Capital City:
Kathmandu

Famous Face

Name: Mira Rai

Famous For: champion trail runner and mountain runner

Religions

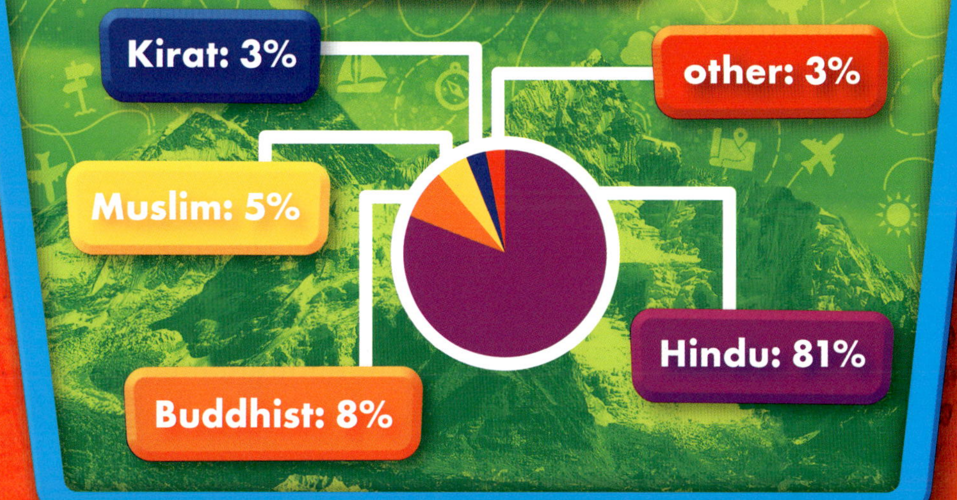

Top Landmarks

Boudha Stupa

Chitwan National Park

Pashupatinath Temple

Glossary

celebrate—to do something special or fun for an event, occasion, or holiday

culture—the beliefs, arts, and ways of life in a place or society

festival—a time or event of celebration

folk music—the traditional music of the people in a country or region

glaciers—massive sheets of ice that cover large areas of land

Hindu—related to a religion that began in India

monsoon—related to winds that change direction each season; monsoons can bring heavy rain.

plains—large areas of flat land

range—a group of mountains

temples—buildings used for religious purposes

traditions—customs, ideas, or beliefs handed down from one generation to the next

trek—to travel on foot for long distances

To Learn More

AT THE LIBRARY

Burbank, Jon. *Nepal*. Buffalo, N.Y.: Cavendish Square Publishing, 2024.

Osborne, Mary Pope. *Sunlight on the Snow Leopard*. New York, N.Y.: Random House, 2022.

Rathburn, Betsy. *Exploring Mount Everest*. Minneapolis, Minn.: Bellwether Media, 2023.

ON THE WEB

FACTSURFER

Factsurfer.com gives you a safe, fun way to find more information.

1. Go to www.factsurfer.com.
2. Enter "Nepal" into the search box and click 🔍.
3. Select your book cover to see a list of related content.

Index

The images in this book are reproduced through the courtesy of: Emad Aljumah, front cover; lumen-digital, front cover; Lulla, p. 3; Issara, pp. 4-5; Thomas Dutour, p. 6; Daniel Prudek, pp. 6-7; quickshooting, pp. 8-9; bijaya gautam, p. 9; Rahul, pp. 10-11; Mikhail Blajenov, p. 11 (snow leopard); Danita Delimont, p. 11 (gharial); Thenuji, p. 11 (red panda); vickey, p. 11 (Indian pangolin); hadynyah/ Getty Images, p. 12; HamsterMan, pp. 12-13; NARESH SHRESTHA, p. 14; Vipula Samarakoon/ Alamy, pp. 14-15; Nabaraj Regmi, pp. 15, 16 (*sel roti*); OliverFoerstner, p. 16 (*dal bhat*); SMDSS, p. 16 (*momos*); SMDSS, p. 16 (*thukpa*); ai_yoshi, p. 17; AP Tolang, p. 18; Ilya Sviridenko, pp. 18-19; daboost, p. 20 (flag); SOPA Images/ Getty Images, p. 20 (Mira Rai); jon_chica, p. 22 (Boudha Stupa, Pashupatinath Temple); rpbmedia, p. 21 (Chitwan National Park); Robin, p. 22.